Let's Go to China!

Written by Madeline Lewis

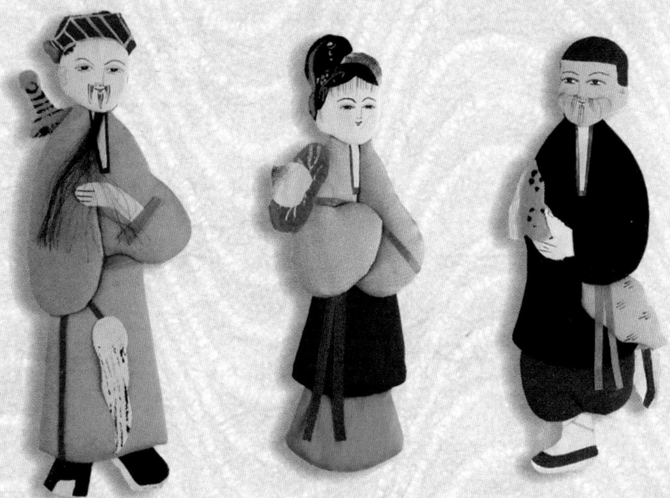

Celebration Press

Parsippany, New Jersey

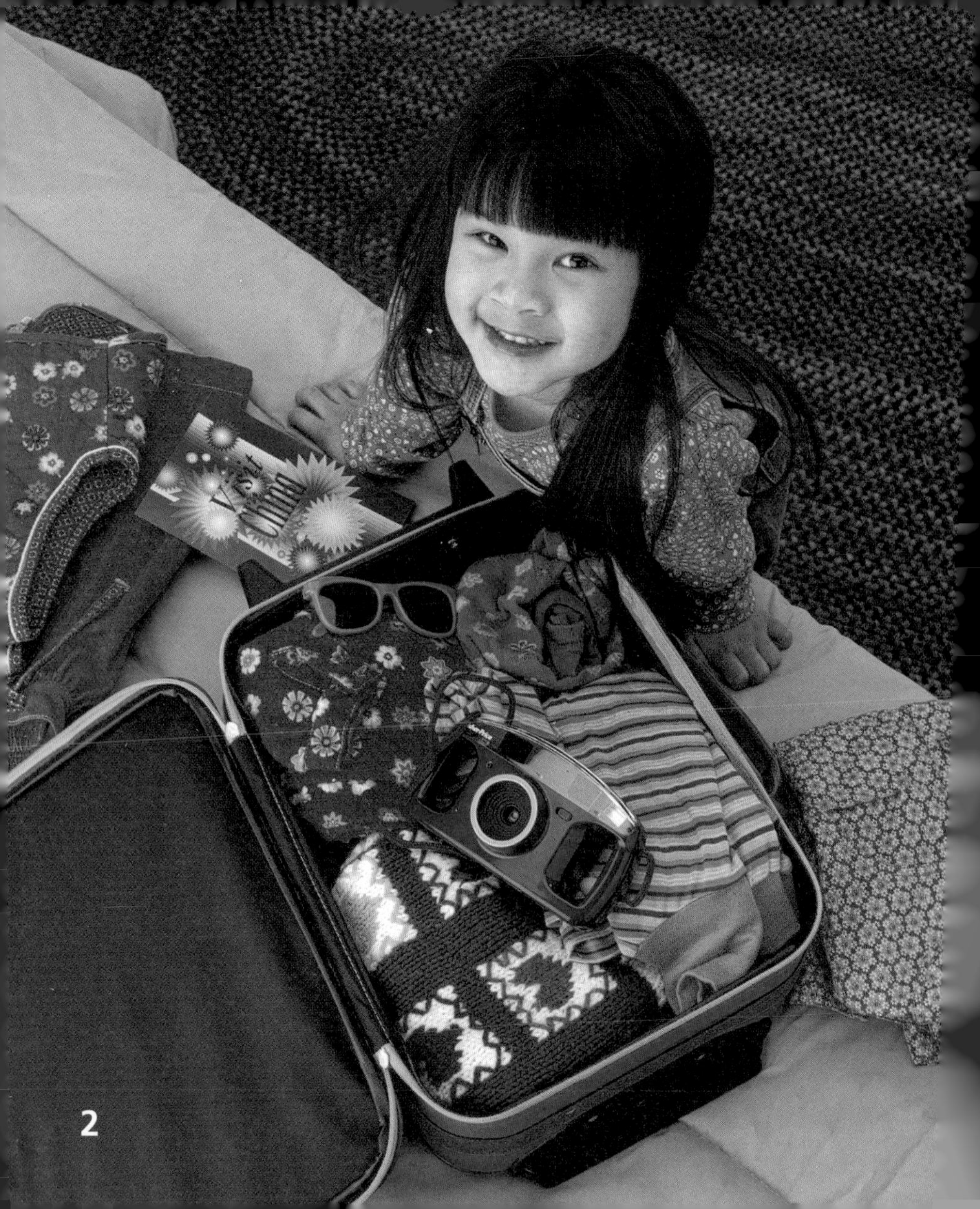
Visit China

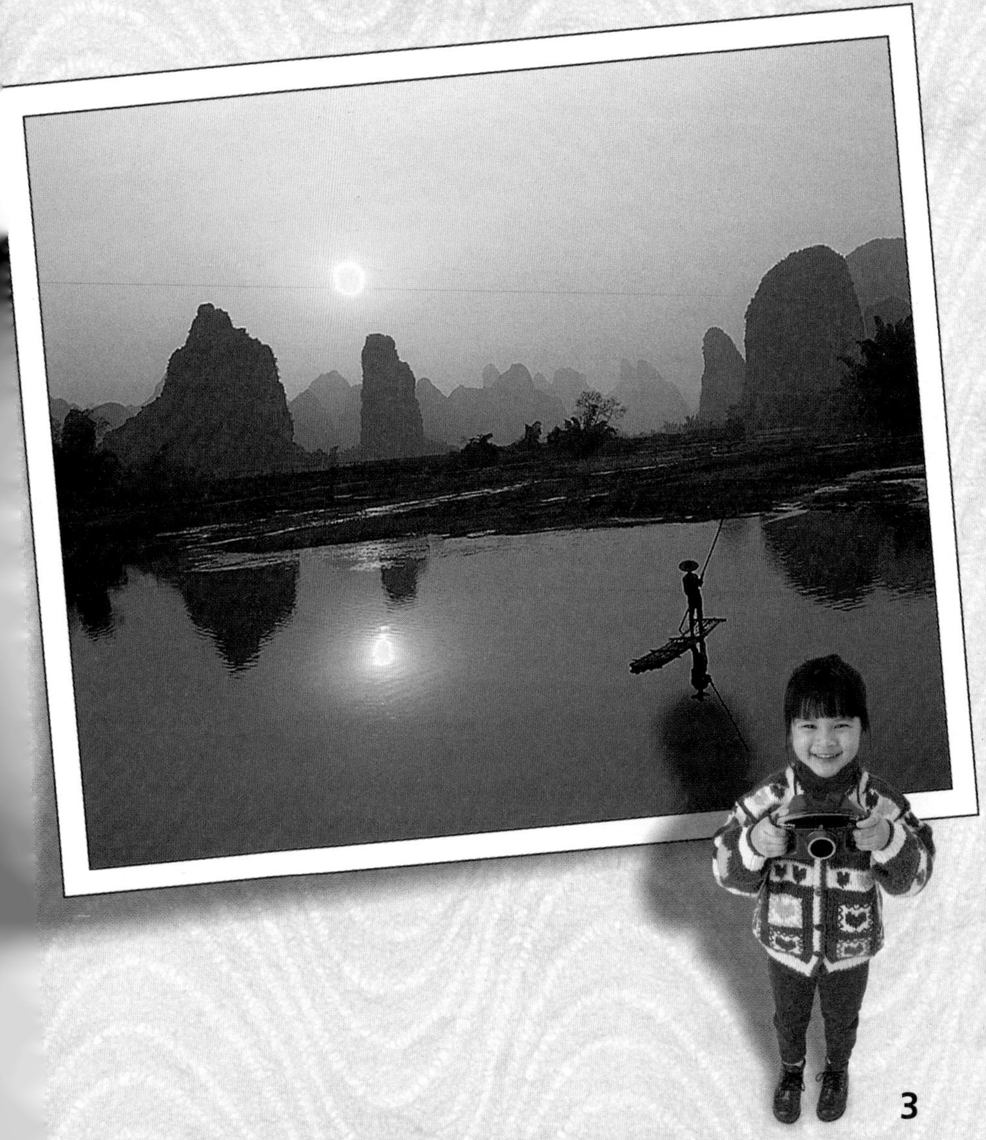

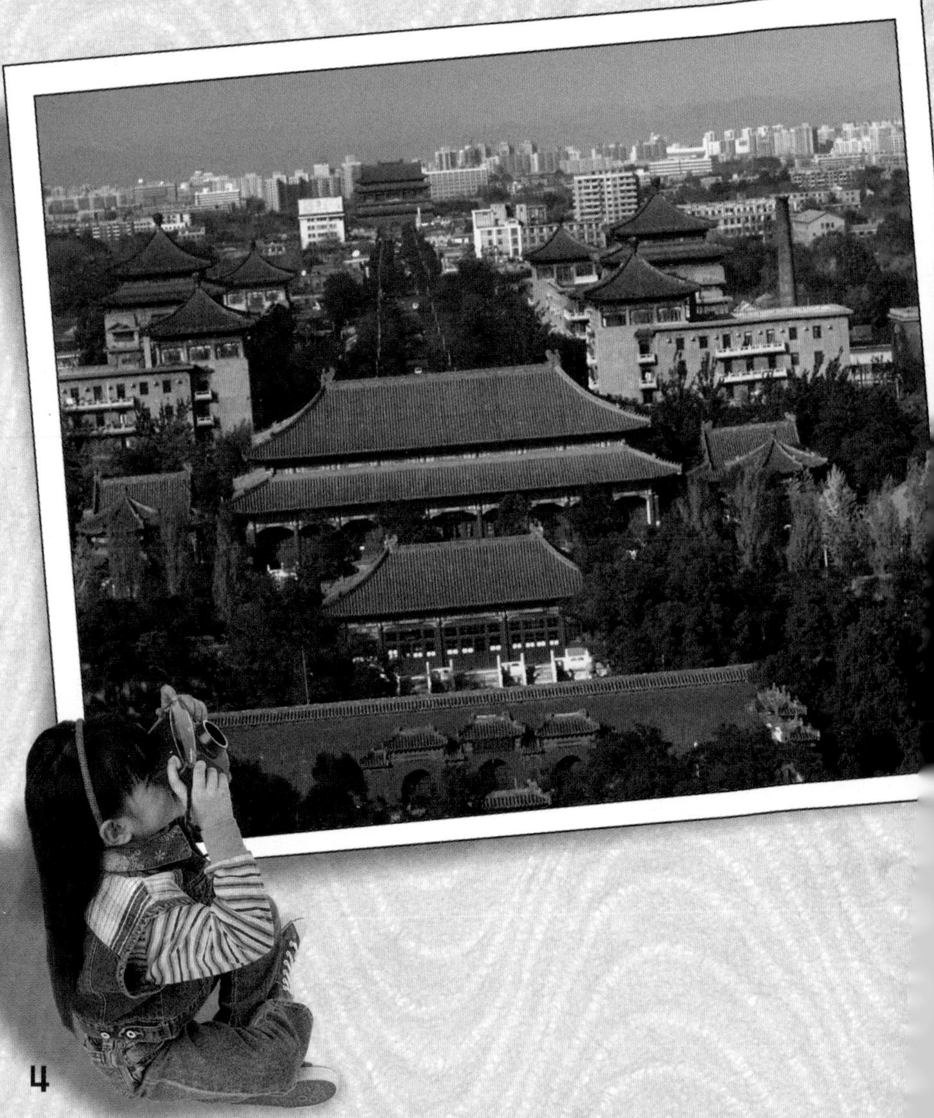

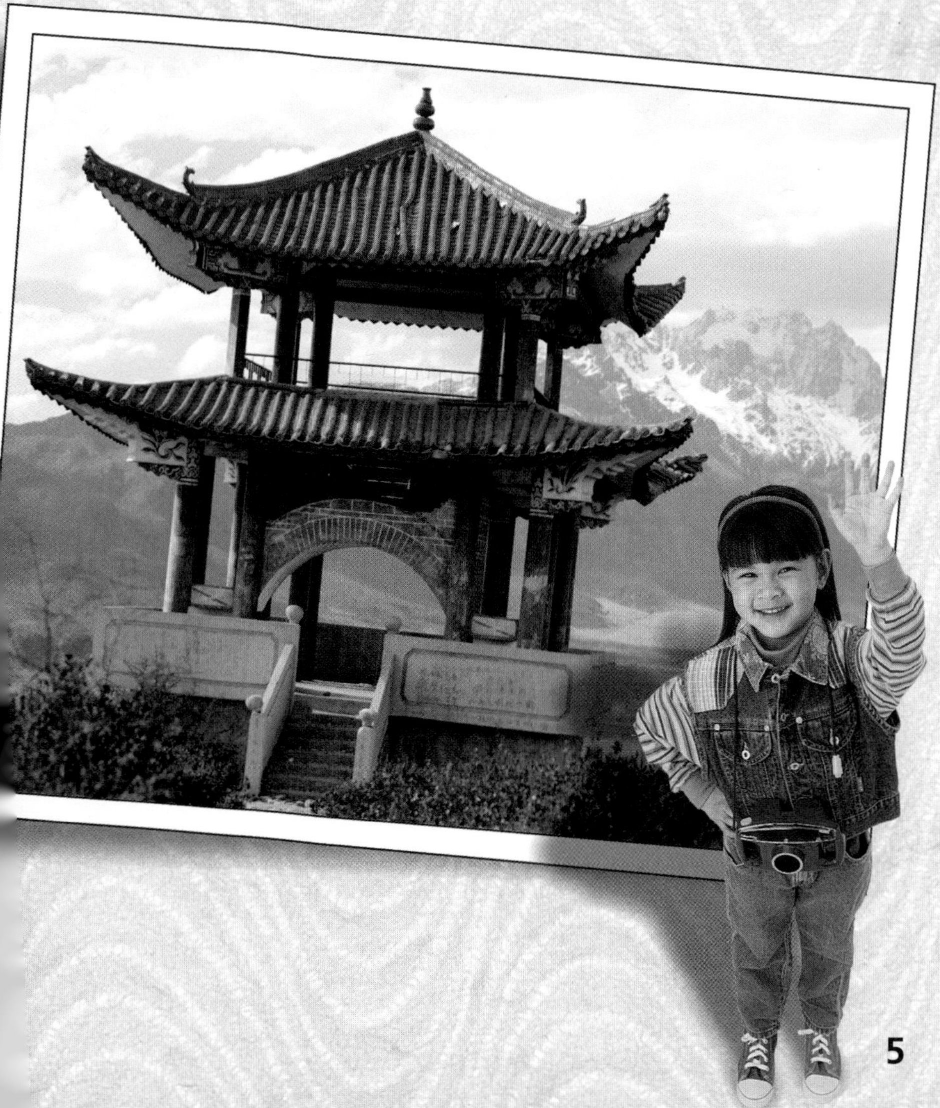

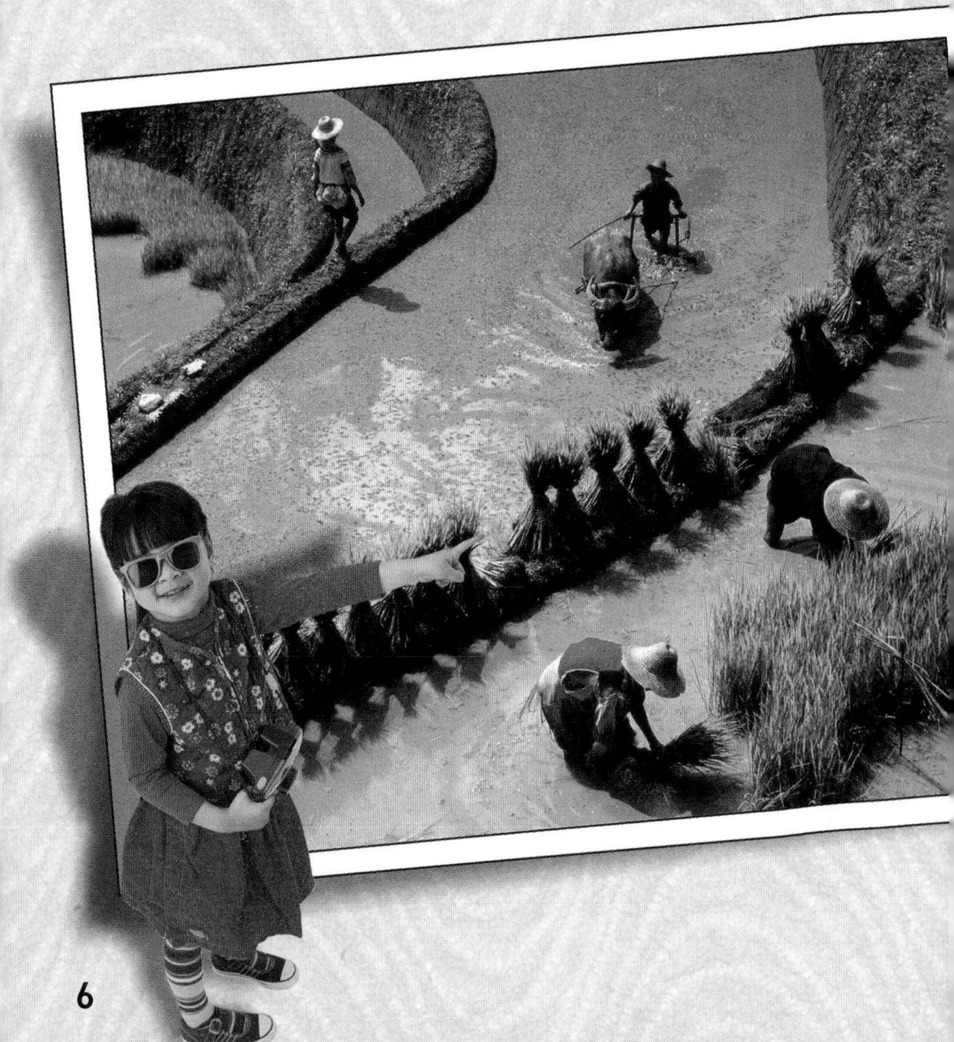

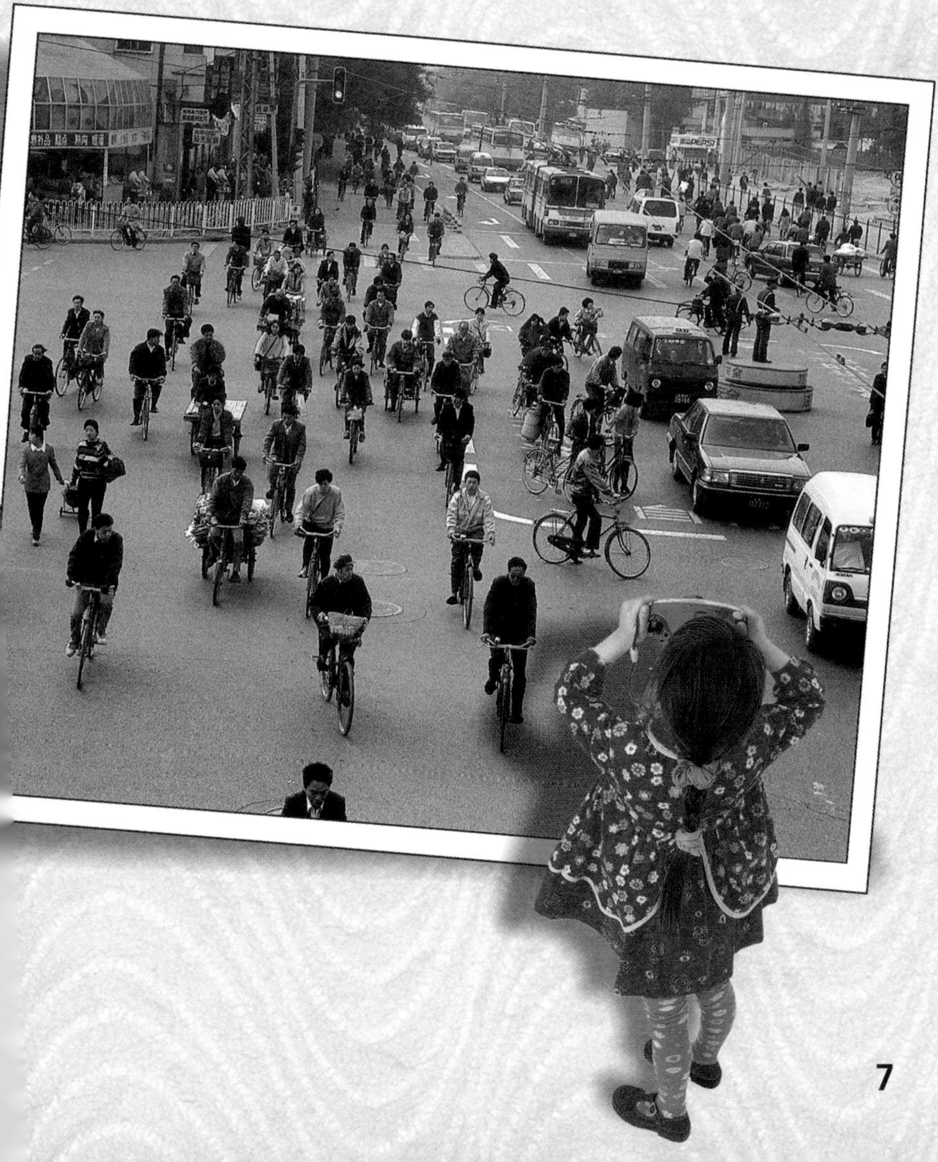
PEPSI

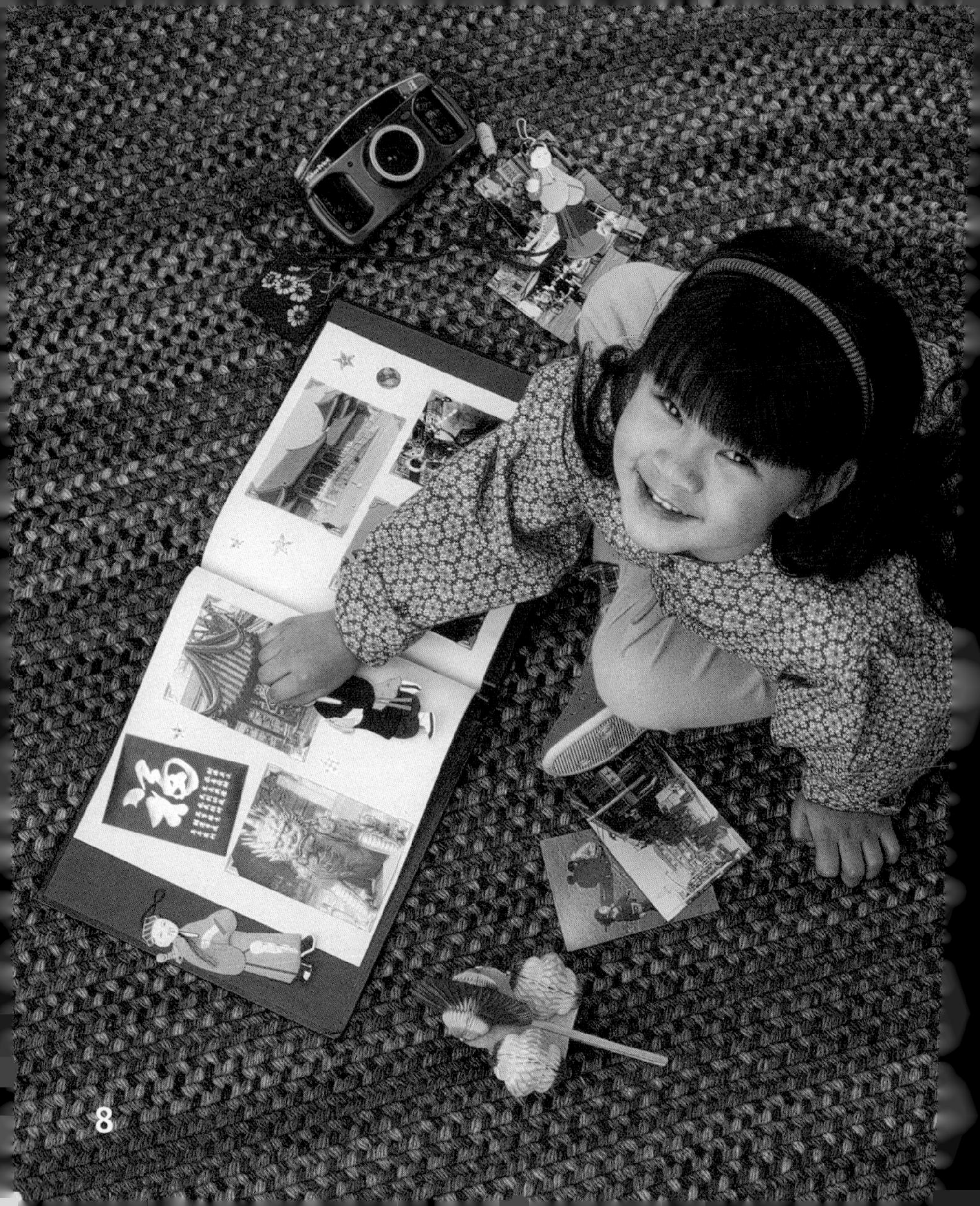